Past Life Prompts

A Journal of Memory Work

About the Author

M. Belanger is the author of over forty books on magick and the occult, including *The Psychic Vampire Codex* and *The Dictionary of Demons.* Founder of the magickal group House Kheperu (1996), Belanger has taught energy work, psychic development, and past life work for over thirty years. One of the only openly intersex people working in US television, Belanger is widely recognizable for appearances on shows like Paranormal State, Portals to Hell, and Paranormal Lockdown. An ENNIE award-winning game designer, Belanger also crafts journaling roleplaying games (TTRPGs) that blend magick, ritual, meditation, and play.

Past Life Prompts

A Journal of Memory Work

M. Belanger

Hardcover ISBN: 978-1-964537-61-0
Library of Congress Control Number on file.

Published by:
Crossed Crow Books, LLC
518 Davis St, Suite 205
Evanston, IL 60201
www.crossedcrowbooks.com

Printed in the United States of America.
IBI

Other Books by M. Belanger

The Dictionary of Demons

The Psychic Vampire Codex: A Manual of Magick and Energy Work

The Psychic Energy Codex: A Manual for Awakening Your Subtle Senses

The Ghost Hunter's Survival Guide: Protection Techniques for Encounters with the Paranormal

The Little Book of Wicked Spells: Binding and Retribution Magick

Walking the Twilight Path: A Gothic Book of the Dead

Table of Contents

Instructions....1

Why Explore Past Lives?....3

Validity of Memories....9

On Memory and Trauma....11

Memory Prompts....15

Final Reflections....295

Instructions

Flip randomly through this book. Wherever you stop, read the prompt. Then, set a timer for ten minutes. Use the front and back of that page to write your response to the prompt. Alternately, you may use a single loose sheet of paper for your response if you do not want to write directly in this book.

You can respond to the same prompt multiple times and potentially get different results depending on the memory that emerges. If you don't want to revisit prompts, consider making a small mark next to the ones you've already answered. Additionally, mark any prompts you may want to skip.

Your rules as you write:

- You can skip any prompt for any reason.
- You do not have to use full sentences in your response.
- You do not have to fill the entire space.
- Your response does not have to make "sense."
- You may draw pictures or symbols as your response.
- Record the first thing that comes to mind.
- Stop once the timer is up.

If you linger on the prompt for more than two minutes and nothing useful comes, close the book and do something else. If you want to come back to the journal that same day, choose a different prompt.

You will get the best results from this journal if you try not to overthink when writing your responses. Go with your first reaction to the question and resist the urge to analyze or edit while you are working (you can do all the analysis you want once you have something recorded on the page).

If nothing comes, or you feel uncomfortable for any reason, don't try to force a response. Some prompts may steer you toward events or issues you aren't ready to confront. Go at your own pace and consider revisiting difficult prompts later if you feel your situation has changed.

Techniques like free association, trance, or automatic writing are helpful but not necessary when doing this work. Although designed for past life work, these prompts can also be used to examine events from your current life. Do so gently, as many of the prompts lean into potentially difficult experiences.

Why Explore Past Lives?

Past life work is most useful when you approach it to better understand who you are right now. Everything in your past has led to this moment, so what are you going to do with it now that you're here?

To this end, the prompts in this journal are crafted to explore moments of strong emotion, the connections we make with people important to us, and the choices whose consequences we may carry even lifetimes after the fact. Sensory triggers for memory also play a role but are generally used to propel the reader toward those critical emotional events.

Your reactions to these prompts may not definitively reveal that you lived a life as a peasant in sixteenth-century France, but they can unearth the emotional themes lingering from your previous experiences. Over time, patterns and cycles emerge that can help guide you toward healing or choosing differently in this current life.

Assessing Your Responses: Sensory Language

When you first respond to a prompt, it's important to immerse yourself as thoroughly as possible in the experience. Try not to edit, question, or analyze what the prompt inspires as you record it. Analysis comes after—ideally once you've had a chance to do something else and separate yourself emotionally from the experience.

When you come back to examine your response, look for patterns that reveal how these memories present for you. The first—and simplest—pattern to spot is your sensory language. We live in bodies wired to interpret our environments through physical senses, and each of us tends to favor one or two of these senses over the others. This bias emerges in our language when we articulate our experiences. Some of us are preferentially visual. Some of us favor sound. Others gravitate to scent, and so on.

Don't limit yourself to the standard five physical senses. Even without considering extra-sensory abilities, humans process their environments through more than simply sight, scent, taste, hearing, and touch. Consider that, when we talk about the *feel* of an experience, we are generally not talking about physical texture, but it is sensory language all the same, and it tells you a lot about how you process the world.

We reveal our sensory bias through the language we unconsciously use when reporting our experiences. With this in mind, go over what you recorded for the prompt and circle all of the instances where you use sensory language such as "I *see* a person" or "I *feel* tension in the room." It may help to make a separate document and organize all of these words into columns so you can better see at a glance how many sight-related words and metaphors you tend to use versus sound, scent, etc. Keep in mind that you may not have enough material in one response to show a pattern, but after responding to multiple prompts, you will start to get an idea of what senses tend to appeal most strongly to you through repetitions in language.

This tendency is important for three main reasons:

First, this pattern will likely repeat itself both in past life and present life memories. Consistency in how you describe your experiences can help differentiate between genuine memories and a story you're embellishing simply because you feel obligated to fill space (this can easily happen unconsciously, as so many of us are trained to please—we seek approval even when it's only from a book).

Second, our favored senses can form a powerful bridge into memory. For example, once you know that you focus first and foremost on the tactile sensation of the world around you, you can use that to pull yourself more completely into a memory. Start with the feel of fabric under your fingers, then ask yourself what you're wearing and why.

Third, our favored sense(s) also reveal what senses we tend to overlook. For most people, smells are a powerful memory trigger, but if scent happens to be at the bottom of your list, it might not be important enough for you to remember what someone's perfume smelled like. Prompts that appeal to a sense you don't resonate with are less likely to inspire a genuine response. If you know you have trouble connecting with your nose, you will know you can skip a scent-based prompt when it comes up—or understand going in that you might not get much out of it.

Assessing Your Responses: Your Style of Memory

Once you've cracked the code of your sensory language, it's time to dig into your overall style of memory. Your sensory biases are a part of this, but they're only the beginning.

Memory is a vast and varied thing. All of us have different elements we tend to remember from each experience. Some of us focus on how an event made us feel, even when details about the event itself remain hazy. Some have vivid recollections of a person's appearance but consistently blank on names. Still others have a clear sense of when an event played out—even to the point of accurately recalling the day of the week—while others struggle to put recollected events into any semblance of chronological order.

Barring severe changes to our mental function, our style of memory tends to remain consistent across the decades. And, in defiance of memory as a purely physical function, our style of memory tends to hold across past lives as well.

To begin identifying your style of memory, first think back to your memories of early childhood. These will tell you a lot about how memory works for you. Are your memories of your earliest years incomplete and hazy? Do you have moments that stand out with startling clarity? Do you mostly recall feelings you had, music you learned, little triumphs where you received supportive praise? Do you have memories of people with no other context? Do you have a sense of chronology or is it like a mess of unmarked photos?

All of these details contribute to an understanding of your unique style of memory. The underpinning structure of your style of memory comes down to this: *we tend to remember experiences we deem important enough to hold onto.* The trick is to figure out what "important" means to you specifically.

Here again, language cues can be helpful.

When attempting to assess your style of memory, first go back over your response to the prompts and take note of how often you are concerned with reporting events from your interior reality (what you think, feel, imagine, and want in the moment) versus exterior reality (who you are with, what you are doing, how your body feels, and what's happening in your environment). This offers insight into whether you tend to place more value on your interior world or your exterior world. Value, of course, doesn't mean that one of these is better than the other, only that you personally tend to pay more attention in one of these directions. As with your sensory bias, it also reveals that you are *less likely* to pay attention to the other options. A person who is richly immersed in their interior world may not even notice key details in their physical environment.

Once you have a good idea of which direction your focus tends to favor, begin to narrow details down even further. If you are someone immersed in your interior world, do your descriptions of events favor language related to emotion? Perhaps you are goal-oriented, so you mostly recall what you're planning to do or reflecting on what you have done. A creative person may remember the art they want to work on with more immediacy than the moment that inspired the art in the first place.

Again, it's all in what we find important—and "important" is relative to each person's preferences, experiences, and goals.

Broadly, your style of memory can reveal:

- If you are more likely to remember interior or exterior occurrences
- If or how you remember people (faces? Names? What they were wearing?)
- What types of experiences you are more likely to retain (happy ones? Sad ones? Times you were praised?)
- Whether or not you retain details about your body
- What elements of your physical environment catch your attention (architectural details? Geography? The weather?)

This is by no means a complete list, but it gives you a place to start.

Your style of memory is important because it reveals patterns and themes in what matters to you across lifetimes. This can help you understand cycles or ruts you find yourself in right now and potentially offers insight into how you might change those, should you want to. It can also help you better understand the preferences and motivations you carry on a fundamental level. Armed with this understanding, you can make better choices based on what you actually want out of life, as opposed to what you might be doing only because of circumstance, training, or obligation.

Validity of Memories

A vital aspect of understanding your patterns of memory, both sensory and otherwise, is assessing the validity of your recollections, particularly when responding to these prompts.

By its very nature, memory is imperfect. But if your response to a prompt deviates significantly from what you've come to understand as your style of memory, that's a cue that it may not be a memory at all. Accidental fictions happen easily, especially if we're trying too hard, have high expectations for our performance, or try to fit our experience into pre-conceived notions of what our past lives *should* look like.

The good news is even accidental fiction can tell you something about yourself: themes you find appealing, goals you hope to accomplish, how you like to think of yourself, and how you would prefer to be seen. All of these are useful data points along your path to self-development. However, if accuracy is your goal, here are some things to look for in false or embellished narratives:

- Inconsistent with your style of memory
- Too elaborate, perfect, or complete
- Centers you in a grandiose fashion (for good or ill)

- Includes sensory detail you normally overlook
- A high-stakes narrative; epic and world-changing
- Contains no ambiguity; an unlimited point of view, power, or expertise
- Matches a story you may have seen, heard, or read before

What should you do if the "memory" you just wrote hits some or all of these?

Keep it and note where and how it deviates from the memories you've assessed as more accurate. Does it start with a little nugget of recollection and then veer into fabrication? That provides useful information: what spun you off track? Maybe the prompt didn't inspire anything, but you felt obligated to put *something* down. As you pushed, your unconscious supplied a story to fill the space. Alternately, the prompt may have triggered a memory you are not emotionally ready to unpack, and, as a way to insulate your psyche, your unconscious provided a rollicking tale to distract and deflect from the discomfort. Sometimes a grandiose tale is a metaphor for a genuine memory, but there's a lot of sound and fury to peel away before you get to the real message. Understanding why some part of you felt the need to dress it up can expose unresolved traumas, rigidities in your worldview, and conflicts with your current sense of self. If you can learn to recognize your problems, you can guard against them in the future—or at least better identify when they influence your results in further exercises.

Ideally, your journaling process in this book will not merely be about unearthing past life memories: it is also about learning to differentiate between memory and wish-fulfillment, harmless little fictions, and the lies we tell ourselves to deflect from troublesome truths. All of this is only important in what it reveals to you about you.

Lives come and go. People, movements, and whole cultures are forgotten as the centuries grind them to dust. In the end, it's all about what we carry forward and how we use it here and now.

On Memory and Trauma

As you work through this book, you will notice many of the prompts lean into difficult or dangerous situations. There are mentions of war, death, family separation, and personal loss. Not everything is doom and gloom, of course: these challenging prompts are peppered among moments of joy, creation, friendship, and personal triumph.

Lives are a sum of many experiences—light-hearted and low, the bright and the harrowing. But as anyone who's lived through it can tell you, trauma sticks with us in a very particular way that positive memories often don't.

When diving into past life work, one unavoidable trauma is death. Although we sometimes pass peacefully (or even with a sense of relief), death is often an incandescent moment of loss, pain, regret, and fear of what comes next.

If you have lived before, you have also died before, and you will always carry some portion of that experience. Memories of traumatic events are processed differently, and how your deaths present to you will tell you a lot about how you process traumatic memories in general.

Memories anchored to trauma often deviate from our normal style of memory. They are the exception to all the rules. This is because we process and store our trauma differently from other experiences—in this life and in all others.

Most people will have one of two memory responses to a traumatic event: imprint or erase. Those who imprint their trauma remember the event in punishing detail, often with a clarity and immediacy their other memories lack. These imprinted memories, when accessed, can feel like you are right back in the moment. Time becomes meaningless because the full sensory experience of the traumatic event is frozen in an eternal *now* somewhere deep in your psyche. When that frozen moment surfaces into consciousness (often because of a trigger), it is called a *flashback.*

If you suffer from PTSD, flashbacks can be debilitating. (Ask me how I know.)

The trauma response of erasure is no less troublesome. People who process their trauma through erasure completely suppress the event. They may have a nagging sense of a hole in their memory—lost time, a period of confusion, dissociation, or fugue—but the details are obscure at best. A deep part of their psyche insulates them from ever having to relive the event.

It's important to note we don't choose how we remember our trauma. However, our trauma response tends to be consistent across events. That consistency also reveals a pattern we can track throughout the cycle of previous lives.

For the purpose of this book, knowing whether you are inclined to imprint or erase your trauma can help you better understand your reaction to any prompts that lean into an experience you found traumatic. If you discover a cluster of prompts that always make you shut down (perhaps they have to do with war), they may be pointing to traumatic memories that are held out of reach to cushion you. Now might not be the time to push. If, on the other hand, certain prompts propel you with immediate and uncomfortable clarity into reliving an event, you know that you tend to imprint and can prepare for (or skip over) the prompts that might trigger those intense reactions.

Working through trauma, whether the memories are buried or frozen, is a complex and personal process, and not one to undertake casually. It's useful to have outside guidance. If you can't find a counselor or therapist whom you trust, there are apps and workbooks that can provide essential tools for navigating these most difficult memories.

However you choose to work with your trauma, remember to be gentle with yourself.

Memory Prompts

**This is the scent of home.
What is it like?**

Heads turn as you pass.
What do they see when they look at you?

**You carry a vital message.
Why was it entrusted to you?**

**You love this animal like family.
How did they come to you?**

**You have survived.
What was the cost?**

You look out the nearest window. What do you see?

You wear this every day.
What meaning does it hold for you?

You've worked hard for this victory. How do you celebrate?

Your body grows weak.
What struggles have you endured?

**You sit down to your meal.
What's your favorite food?**

**You must hide or they will find you.
What led to this moment?**

You hold something heavy in your hand. What are you going to do with it?

You have been forced from your job. What was your profession?

It must be here somewhere!
What do you seek?

**Someone leans in and whispers.
Why are they being secretive?**

The wound looks worse than you imagined. What happened?

**You reach for a tool.
What do you plan to build?**

They are arguing again.
What's the disagreement about?

Past Life Prompts

The perfume has a distinctive smell. Who used to wear it?

It rains and rains.
What will this mean for the people living here?

**All your training has led to this.
What do you seek to accomplish?**

**You look up at the sky.
What do you see?**

A child is crying.
Why are they upset?

**You wish you'd said goodbye.
Who do you miss?**

**This is a moment of quiet.
What do you do with your time?**

You hold a length of fabric in your hands. What stands out about it?

You will never have a chance like this again. Why do you hesitate?

In this place, all your needs are met. Where are you?

You hear people singing in the distance. How do you feel about the song?

You are not safe here with your lover. Why?

You need to make room for a guest. How do you prepare your home?

You are dressed in your finest clothes. What is closest to your skin?

A child has come to you for help. What do they need?

You've been given an important task. What's expected of you?

Someone raises their hand to strike you. How do you respond?

You are making something for a loved one. What do they cherish?

**It's time to sleep.
Who else is nearby?**

You've sacrificed so much for this. What do you hope to accomplish?

You want to tell them you love them one last time. Who are they?

**You need more light to see.
What do you reach for?**

You prepare for a very important event. How are you expected to dress?

You are asked to swear your loyalty. What is your response?

You reach for a drinking vessel. What's inside?

**There is a garden nearby.
What grows in it?**

**You smell smoke in the air.
Where is it coming from?**

**You hear the sound of the ocean.
Where are you in relation to the water?**

You have returned home, but something's wrong. Where is everyone?

You know how to make this and make it well. What is it?

It's getting dark soon. Where should you go?

**You have a musical instrument.
How is it played?**

You are cooking.
What supplies do you need?

This constant running exhausts you. Why must you flee?

You're accused of a crime. Did you do it?

**You need to carry water.
What do you use?**

**There is blood everywhere.
What happened?**

Your lover turns their face to yours. What do you notice first?

You hear wild animals in the distance. Are you safe?

This is the most important night of your life. What do you hope to achieve?

**You are on the water.
Where are you headed?**

**Patiently, you track your quarry.
What are you hunting?**

You are being kept against your will. What can you do about it?

**Your home is destroyed.
What is the greatest loss?**

You must report to your superior. How do you approach them?

You learn to write your name. What does the process look like?

You feel the pain of a death-blow. Who or what has struck you down?

You've waited so long for this day. Why are you excited?

**You want the sound to stop.
Where are you?**

**There are flowers all around.
Who planted them?**

You hold a treasured object in your hand. Why is it important to you?

You have never argued like that before. What caused the conflict?

**You pack your belongings.
Why must you move?**

A friend gives you a precious gift. Why did they choose it for you?

You make shelter for the evening. What must you gather first?

You anoint yourself with scented oil. What are you preparing for?

You left home a long time ago. What do you miss most?

A mirror stands before you.
Who do you see?

**You must guard them.
Why is it important?**

A great procession marks a celebration. What do you notice first?

**You study the writing.
Where did you learn how to read?**

You feel exposed.
What led to this moment?

You must make a careful record of this event. Why is it important?

**You would die for them.
Who are you protecting?**

You see a face you recognize. Who are they?

You're on the ground.
What has happened to you?

**The sky is bright with stars.
What catches your attention first?**

**You hate this place.
Why do you stay?**

**Someone grabs you for a kiss.
What do you want to do next?**

The market bustles with people. What are you looking for?

You are being pulled to your feet. What just happened?

You find them very attractive. Why can't you talk to them?

You are building something. What do your hands look like?

No one else has experiences like these. Who can help you understand?

**The information is restricted.
Why do you seek it?**

There won't be enough food this season. Who can you ask for help?

**You sneak in to leave a gift.
Where are you?**

All you can find is a narrow path. Why do you need to follow it?

**You must disguise yourself.
What do you change first?**

You have been sent to work for someone. What is expected of you?

**You used to love this food.
Why can't you find it anymore?**

You must escape with this one thing. What is it?

**You seek a healer.
What do they wear?**

You will always make time for this person. Who are they?

You almost forgot how much you loved this as a child. What is it?

You wear the symbol with pride. What does it represent?

You want so badly to be noticed. Why is it difficult?

**This is your favorite place to visit.
How did you find it?**

**These stairs seem to go on forever.
Where are you headed?**

**This person will teach you.
What do you hope to learn?**

There are dancers at the celebration. How are they dressed?

**You fear it was all for nothing.
Why did you work so hard?**

Your parents say goodbye before you leave. What do they give you?

**You are in a long hallway.
What do you notice about the walls?**

Doing this makes you feel attractive. Why?

You've lost someone very close to you. What happened?

**You look down at your uniform.
What are you wearing?**

**You hear music in the next room.
What are your plans for the evening?**

When you want someone to understand you, you share this. What is it?

You are fighting with someone you once loved. What is the fight about?

It has been a long and difficult journey. Who travels with you?

**A door stands before you.
What is it made of?**

**This is a cause worth fighting for.
What can you do to help?**

**This is your rite of passage.
What trials have you overcome?**

Someone tells you their deepest secret. How do you react?

**A bright sun hangs in a clear sky.
Where are you going?**

**The world around you is chaotic.
What do you worry about the most?**

**Their attention is making you blush.
Who else knows about this?**

You wake up early.
Why do you feel anxious?

You follow the walkway.
How does it look beneath your feet?

This simple act brings you so much joy. What first inspired it?

You did not give your permission for this. What has happened?

You are in a dark and lonely place. What gives you hope?

You've been promised your favorite treat. What is it?

This marks a transition in your life. What are you about to do?

**The performer wears a mask.
What does it look like?**

You are sitting with your mother. What's your relationship like?

**A great storm rages.
Where will you find shelter?**

This person is incredibly influential. How do you know them?

This is the oldest place you can remember. What do you see when you look up?

**Tears well in your eyes.
What just happened?**

**You have found a hidden passage.
Where does it lead?**

Back home, someone waits for you. Who are they?

You have to hide this thing about yourself. What happens if you don't?

**You enter a lavish home.
How do you know the owner?**

**People seek you out for advice.
How did you come by your expertise?**

**Everything is flooding.
Where are you?**

You are not allowed here.
Why?

**You are supposed to get married.
What is your opinion on the matter?**

**You pound on a locked door.
Why must you get in?**

**A vision startles you.
Who can you safely share it with?**

You have stolen something of great value. What happens if you're caught?

**This is the wildest party.
What are people doing?**

Only those chosen may pass beyond this point. Where are you?

The person who raised you is dying. What do you do at their end?

There is a great structure in the distance. What do you know about it?

You stand in a prison.
What side of the bars are you on?

You've been asked to make an offering. What will you give?

There is a celebration in your honor. Who will be there?

All the other students follow the rules. What about you?

You find yourself in a sacred place. What does it feel like to be here?

**Your partner has left you.
What led to the schism?**

So many people are sick and dying. Who do they seek for help?

**You step out of your home.
What do you see around you?**

**You are deep underground.
How did you get here?**

**A child looks to you for guidance.
Why are you important to them?**

You reach for the nearest weapon. What does it feel like in your hand?

You think you have been here before. What memories does this place carry?

You've already had too much, but you want more. Where are you?

You must provide for your loved ones. What do you do?

**You refuse the order.
Who gave it to you?**

You must get up early for practice. What are you training for?

**You hear a baby crying.
What is the first thing you do?**

**You have been asked to leave.
What will happen if you don't?**

Urgent business calls you from pleasure. What is your job?

Nothing will ever be the same.
What brought the change?

You run your hand along the wall. What's it made of?

You have never felt so happy. Who do you share this with?

**Everything is locked.
How did you get here?**

You have been given an extravagant gift. Why?

You don't think there is another living thing for miles. How did you get here?

The time has come to see your child off. Where are they going?

You are expected to perform soon. How do you prepare?

Someone has gravely insulted you. What do you do?

You are home and surrounded by family. Are you happy here?

This is where you take the dead.
How are you expected to behave?

**You have some time to yourself.
What do you do when you're not working?**

You spend time with your favorite pet. How would you describe your bond?

You have been told you must go to war. How do you feel about fighting?

This place is smaller than you expected. Where do you go first?

You need food.
How do you get it?

**You are expected somewhere.
What must you do when you arrive?**

This person has been a mentor to you. What lessons have they shared?

You never expected to live this long. How do you feel about your life?

You are working in the garden.
What plants do you tend?

**You are surrounded by art and finery.
Do you feel like you belong?**

**You must go on a long journey.
How will you travel?**

**Everything is burning.
What do you run back to save?**

You are told you must kneel. How do you respond?

**You are growing old.
Who will look after you?**

You run along the crooked path. What grows nearby?

This is the safest you have ever felt. Who else is with you?

You stand before a precious icon. What importance does it hold?

**Someone holds your tiny hand.
Where do they lead you?**

Everyone is shouting. What's going on?

**You are certain you are lost.
How did you get here?**

**You are hopelessly in love.
What gifts do you dream of giving them?**

**You lay down your weapons.
Why have you surrendered?**

You look upon your work with pride. Who taught you your craft?

You write something down.
Who needs to see this?

You wake up from a terrible nightmare. What are you afraid of?

It is a privilege to receive this. Why have you been chosen?

**Your family is threatened.
How will you protect them?**

**The crowd is enormous.
What brought all these people together?**

**The pressure is unbearable.
What are you expected to do?**

Someone holds you tenderly.
Why are you together?

**Everything is recorded here.
What are you allowed to take?**

You thought they were lost. Where do you find them?

This was your favorite toy.
How did you play as a child?

**This name is important to you.
When did you first hear it?**

No one will look at you the same way again. What did you do?

You are expected to stay where you are. Why can't you leave?

A person in authority approaches. How do you respond?

**Your prayers have been answered.
Where do you go to worship?**

**This is a simple pleasure.
When did you first enjoy it?**

**You don't want to work any longer.
What happens if you stop?**

You took this when you left home. Why is it precious to you?

Everyone expects you to behave a certain way. Do you?

**It is your turn to pay.
Where are you?**

People are fighting in the streets. What's going on?

You want to spend more time with your lover. What's stopping you?

You hear a voice calling you. What does it say?

**The baby is on the way.
How do you prepare?**

You know this is forbidden. Why do you want it anyway?

You promise to keep them safe. Who are they?

This is your best friend.
What favor do you ask of them?

**You learned this song as a child.
Who taught it to you?**

You can see a light in the distance. What emotions does it inspire?

This is not a popular opinion. Why do you believe it anyway?

You are trying to warn people.
What is about to happen?

**This is the finest work of your life.
What have you created?**

**There are so many people dying.
What brought this calamity?**

**Every day is the same.
What is your routine?**

**You taught them everything.
How do they respond?**

**Justice must be done.
What role do you play?**

You feel calm and far from your body. What is happening around you?

**War is coming.
What must you do?**

**This is your favorite way to relax.
What do you enjoy most?**

This discovery will change peoples' lives. How do you learn about it?

This is a happy time.
What does home look like?

**You feel constantly ignored.
What do people see when they look at you?**

**You value this luxury.
What is it?**

**This is the land you call home.
What does it look like?**

**You must ask permission to see them.
Why is it important?**

**You don't like these clothes.
What do you prefer?**

When you see this landmark, you know you're home. What is it?

You want to lose yourself in their arms. Where do you go for privacy?

Carefully, you record your observations. What are you working on?

**Everyone else enjoys this.
Why is it different for you?**

**You have been traveling all night.
Who do you hope to see once you arrive?**

Everyone's excited about this new invention. How do you feel about it?

The child burns with fever.
How do you help them?

Everyone expects the ceremony to go smoothly. What role do you play?

**Someone shakes you awake.
Where are you?**

**You lied to them.
Why?**

You thought you had lost this forever. What is it?

There is music and dancing.
What are you doing?

**You're in charge now.
Where are you?**

**You are cold and hungry.
Who else is around you?**

You will be an adult soon.
What will be expected of you?

You visit this building almost every day. What is its significance?

**People look to you for a solution.
Why do they hold you in high regard?**

No. It goes against your honor.
What have you been asked to do?

**Everyone is upset about this.
Why aren't you?**

**You have lived a long, rich life.
What is your greatest treasure?**

**You could not save them.
Who were they to you?**

This is where you had your first kiss. What led to it?

**You know the end is near.
Who do you expect to be there when you die?**

This door must remain sealed at all costs. What lies beyond?

Final Reflections

The lingering vestiges of previous lives we carry like crystalline structures within the geodes of our souls are many and varied. Consequently, every entry within this exploratory journal can be revisited with different results. Depending upon which life you tap into and which cycle(s) of your existence you're currently working through, different memories will come to the surface, as will different insights.

Don't hesitate to set this book aside for a while after your initial work-through, only to return later from a new perspective. We contain multitudes and spiritual development is not a straight path, nor is it a journey with a fixed destination. Rather, it is in the exploration itself that we grow, thrive, and deepen ourselves.

Past lives are only one part of this: by looking to the past, we can better understand our present, but if we wish to map the best course into our future, we must do everything in our power to master our present selves as well. Do not gaze only backward. This work—the work of the Self—is holistic and should embrace all aspects of who you are and how you experience the world.

—M. Belanger